THE LITTLE BIG MAN

Rabindranath Tagore
Art by Rajiv Eipe

ΦKATHA

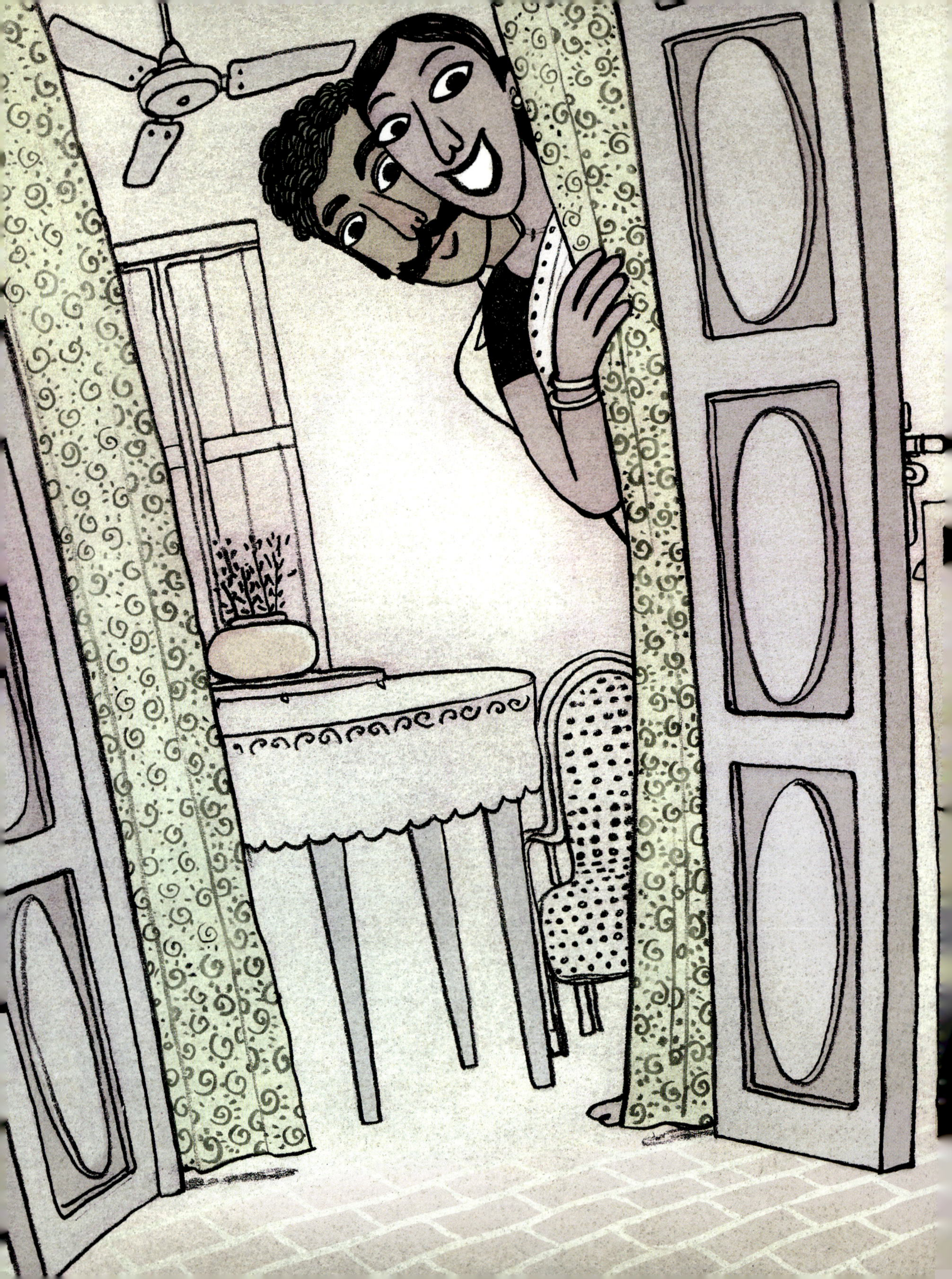

I am small
because I am a little child.
I shall be big
when I am as old as my father.

My teacher will come and say, "It is late, bring your slate and your books."

I shall tell him,
"Do you not know
I am as big as father?
And I must not
have lessons any more."

My teacher will wonder and say, "He can leave his books if he likes, for he is grown up."

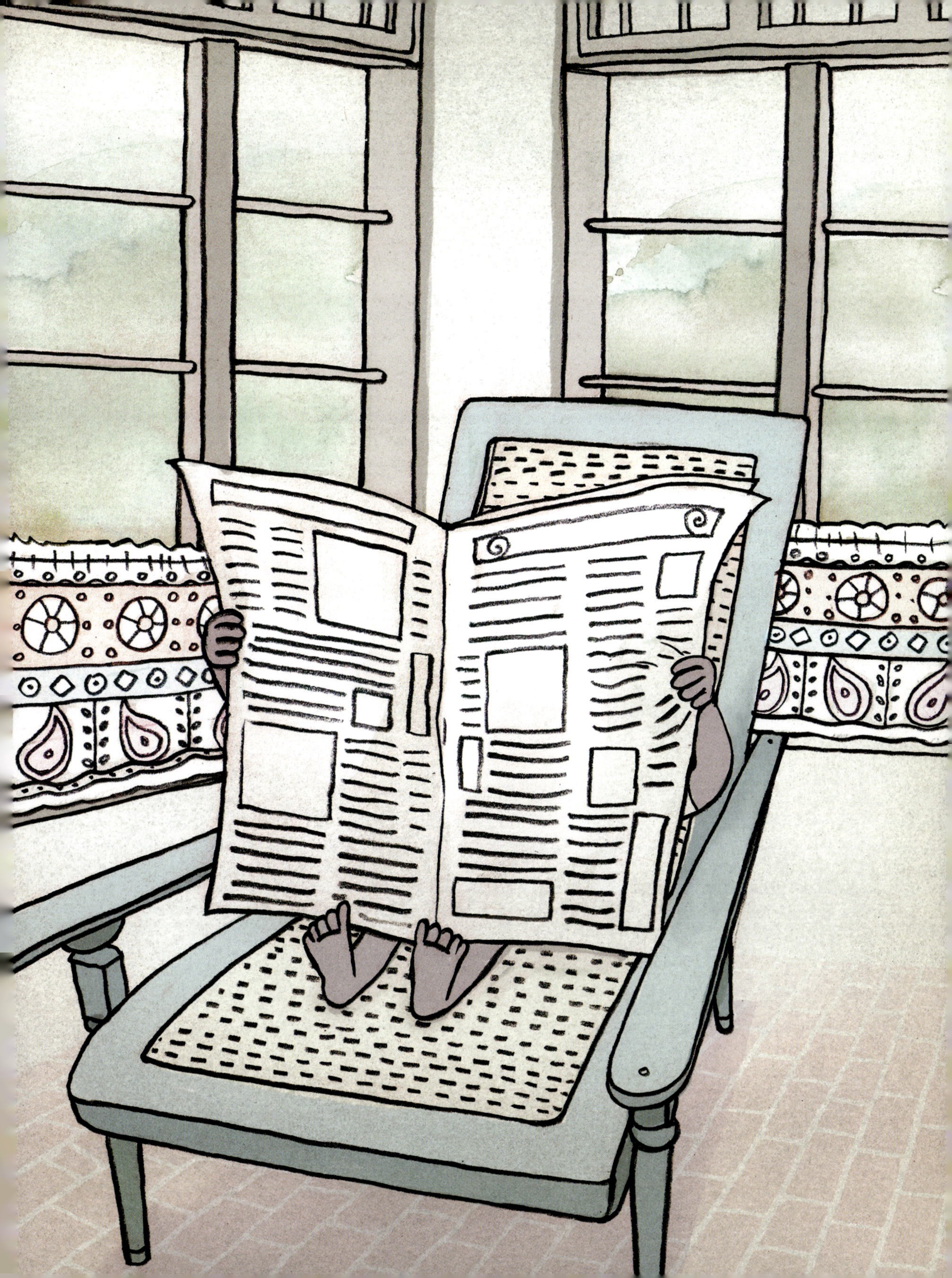

I shall dress myself
and walk to the fair
where the crowd is thick.

My uncle will come rushing up to me and say,
"You will get lost, my boy;
let me carry you."

I shall answer,
"Can't you see, uncle,
I am as big as father?
I must go to the fair alone."

Uncle will say,
"Yes, he can go wherever he likes,
for he is grown up."

Mother will come
from her bath
when I am giving
money to my nurse,
for I shall know
how to open
the box with my key.

Mother will say, "What are you about, naughty child?"

I shall tell her,
"Mother, don't you know,
I am as big as father,
and I must give money to my nurse."

Mother will say to herself,
"He can give money to whom he likes,
for he is grown up."

In the holiday time in October father will come home and, thinking that I am still a baby, will bring for me from the town little shoes and small silken shirts.

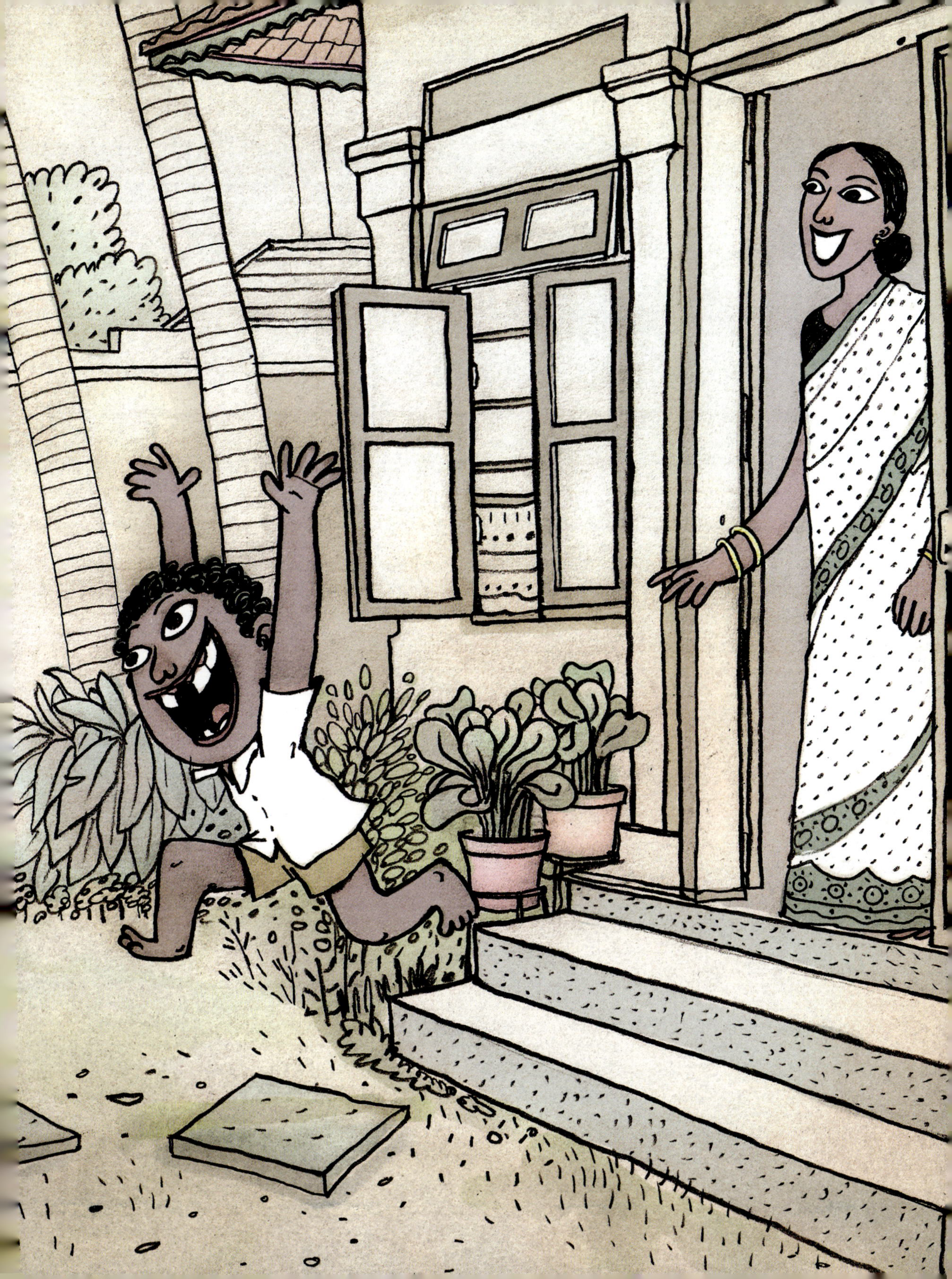

I shall say,
"Father, give them to my dada,
for I am as big as you are."

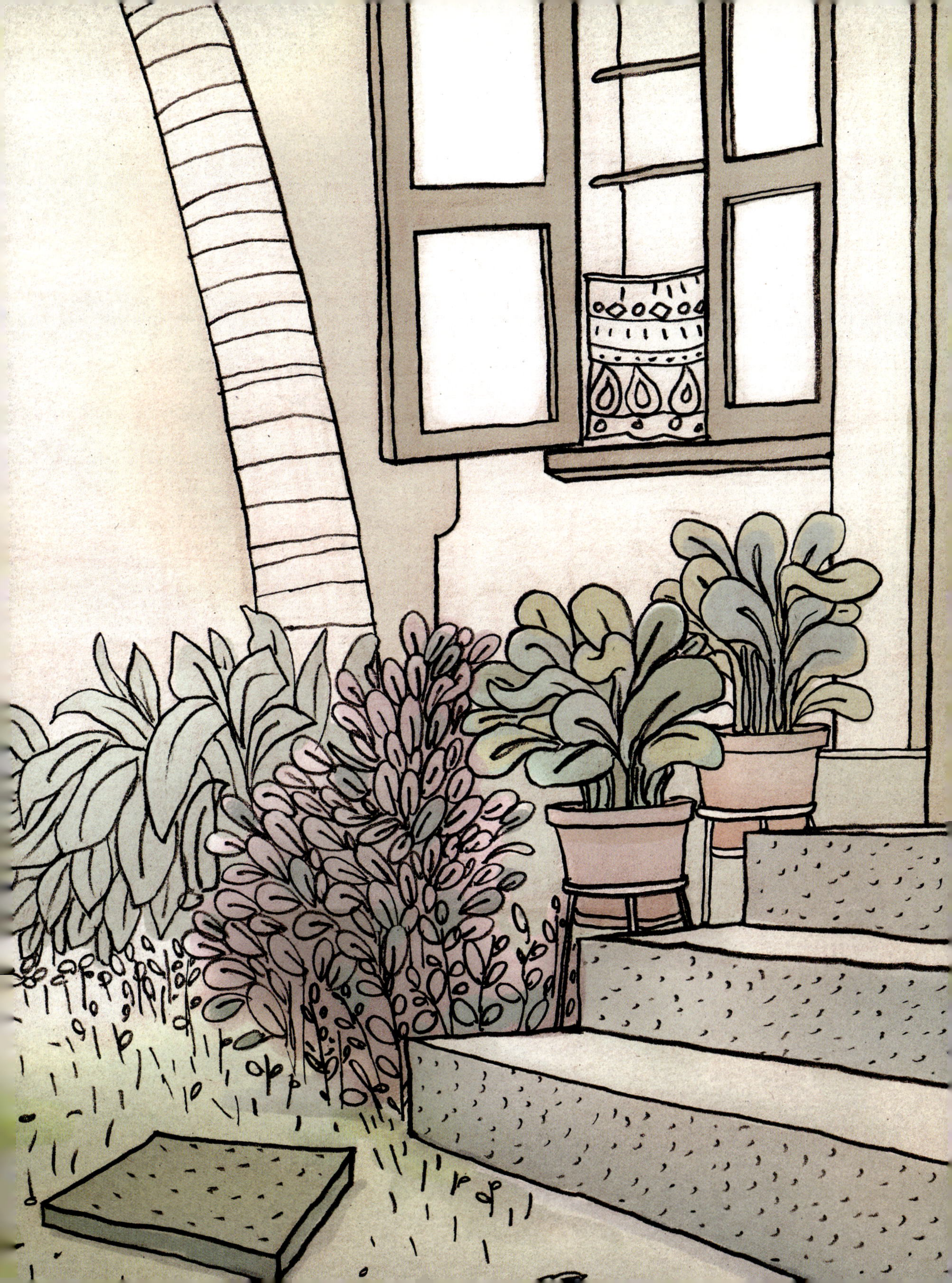

Father will think and say,
"He can buy his own clothes
if he likes,
for he is grown up."

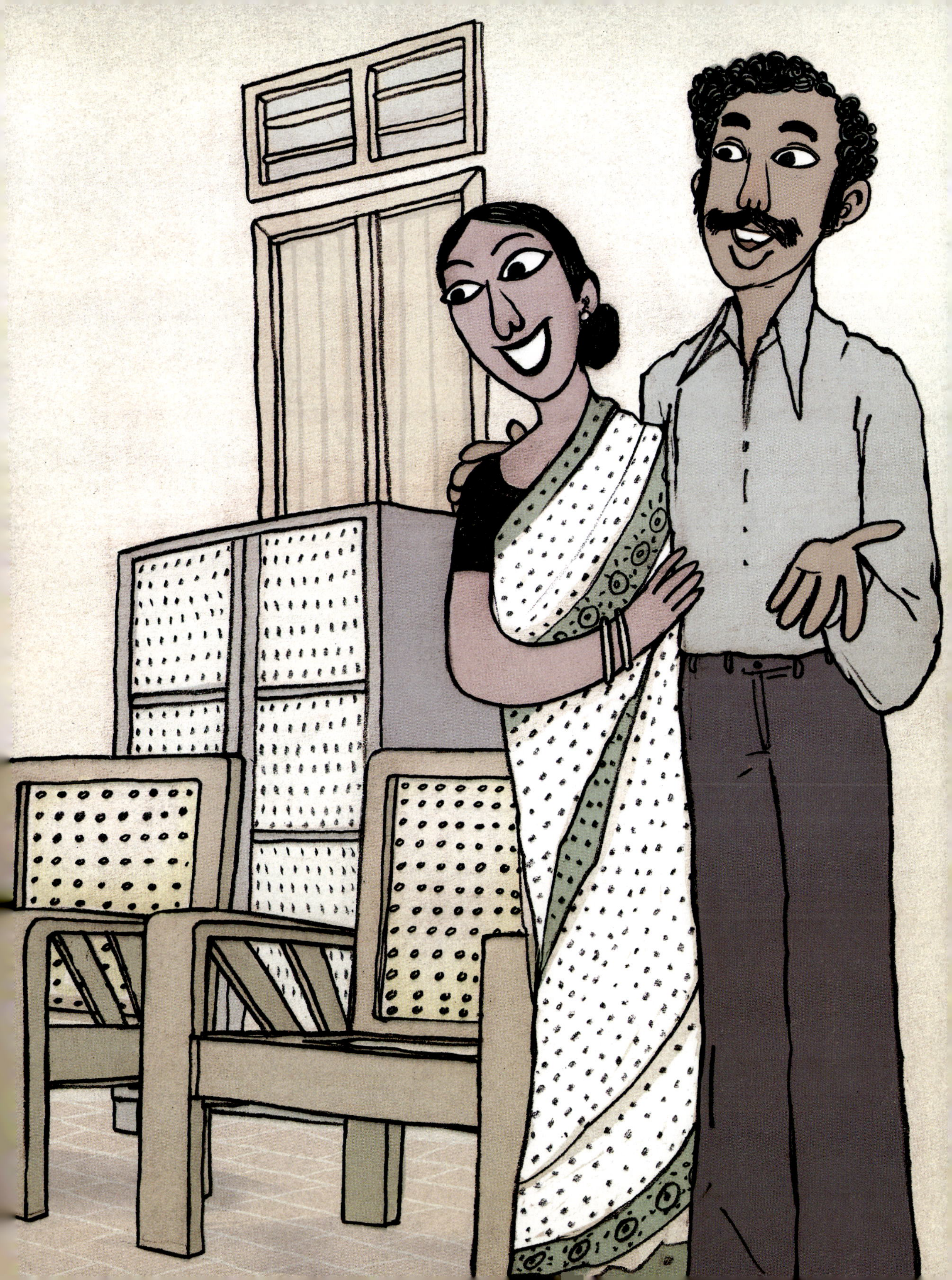

Meet Gurudev

*Where the mind is without fear
and the head is held high,
Where knowledge is free,
Where the world has not been
broken into fragments
By the narrow domestic walls …
Into the heaven of freedom,
my father, let my country awake.*

Do you know who wrote these immortal words? Born 150 years ago, he stood tall in the world of writing and his ideas are still so fresh, so current. He was a writer, painter, musician, poet and storyteller too! Yes, we are talking of Rabindranath Tagore, lovingly called Gurudev.

Gurudev was born on May 7, 1861. His father, Debendranath Tagore, was a Sanskrit scholar. Gurudev's early education was imparted at home. In school, while others use to learn their lessons, he would slip into more exciting world of dreams. The only degrees he ever received were honorary ones, bestowed late in life. He wrote his first poem when he was seven. At the age of seventeen, his first book of poems was published which surprised him to no end.

He later went to England to study law. He always believed that education is the freedom of imagination. In 1901, he founded an international university called *Shantiniketan* or Abode of Peace, which brought out priceless talents like Indira Gandhi, Satyajit Ray and Amartya Sen. Gurudev was a true patriot; he supported the national movement and wrote the lyrics of the *Jana Gana Mana*, which is India's national anthem. He gave the name *Mahatma* to Gandhiji.

He wrote 3,000 poems, 2,000 songs, 8 novels, 40 volumes of essays and short stories and 50 plays. He was awarded the Nobel Prize in Literature for his collection of well-known poems *Gitanjali* (Song Offerings). Many of Gurudev's stories have also been made into films.

Rajiv Eipe studied Fine Arts at Sir J. J. School of Art before he went to study Animation Film Design at the National Institute of Design, Ahmedabad. Rajiv lives in Mumbai where he mainly does animation and graphics for Television and secretly wishes to drive a taxi for a living.

KATHA

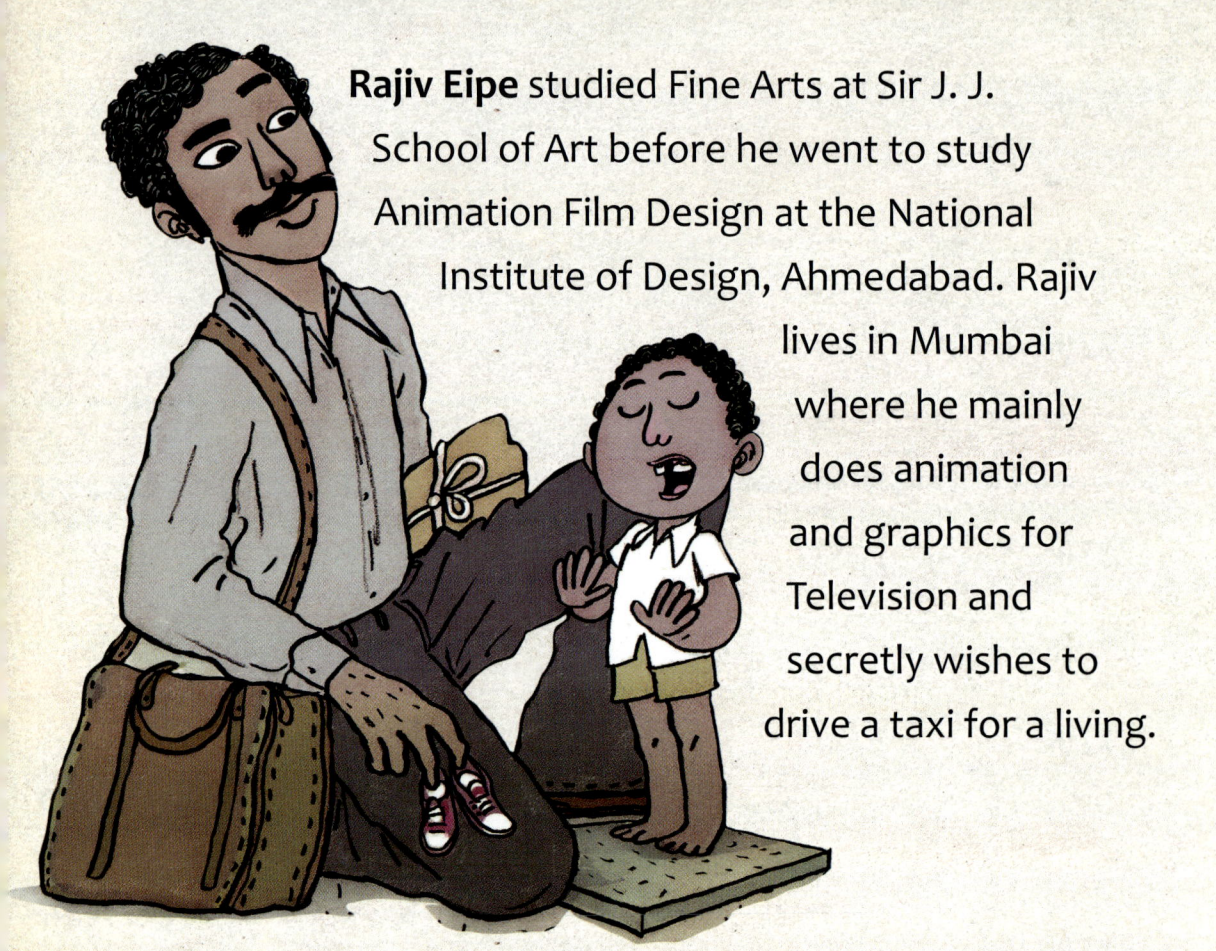

First published © Katha, 2011
Copyright © Katha, 2011
Text copyright © Katha, 2011
Illustrations copyright © Rajiv Eipe, 2011
All rights reserved. No part of this book may be reproduced or utilized in any form without the prior written permission of the publisher.
Printed at RaveIndia, New Delhi
ISBN 978-81-89934-81-1

KATHA is a registered nonprofit devoted to enhancing the joys of reading amongst children and adults. Katha Schools are situated in the slums and streets of Delhi and tribal villages of Arunachal Pradesh.
A3 Sarvodaya Enclave, Sri Aurobindo Marg
New Delhi 110 017
Phone: 4141 6600 . 4182 9998 . 2652 1752
Fax: 2651 4373
E-mail: marketing@katha.org, Website: www.katha.org

Ten per cent of sales proceeds from this book will support the quality education of children studying in Katha Schools.
Katha regularly plants trees to replace the wood used in the making of its books.

First Reprint 2013